Moms Letting Go
Without Giving Up

7 Steps to Self-Recovery

D1478254

Michelle Weidenbenner

Please join the mom movement to ruin your son's or daughter's "using" career.

Join our confidential and supportive Facebook (FB) group at MomsLettingGo. Be a part of this Mighty Mom Movement.

Surround yourself with the comforting arms of other moms who want to take charge of their lives and "let go with love—and without giving up."

Your child is worth your fight!

Note: The suggestions in this book apply to adults (at least 18 years old)

ISBN: 978-1-7333810-0-0 e-book
ISBN: 978-1-7333810-1-7 paperback

Printed in the United States of America.

Cover Design by 100Covers.com
Interior Design by FormattedBooks.com

This book is dedicated to the moms who have lost loved ones to addiction. Your children mattered. I pray that moms everywhere will join in solidarity to honor your children's legacies by bringing awareness to this disease and helping to remove the stigma of mental illness. Together we can bring hope to the afflicted.

Blessed are those who mourn, for they will be comforted.
Matthew 5:4 NIV

CONTENTS

**Every flower that has bloomed had
to go through a whole lot of dirt to get there!**

WELCOME

When a flower doesn't bloom, it's because something is lacking in its environment. Until we nourish and nurture the flower's surroundings, it won't grow.

You are the same.

You are a seed waiting to sprout and blossom into a beautiful flower. But first, you need a guide to show you what kind of environment will help you thrive.

I'm honored to be your guide.

I'm Michelle, the mother of a recovering, addicted loved one. I know your pain. Even though my son and daughter-in-law's drug of choice, story, and life is different than your son's or daughter's, I assure you that I have probably felt the same things that you're going through or have been through.

This is hell!

I'm not a counselor or a psychologist. I'm a mom who cares about the health of other moms, like you. I want to be the person you need, the one I didn't have when I started on my long mom-of-an-addict journey.

WELCOME TO THE MIGHTY MOMS CLUB

Our focus is how to ruin our children's "using" career and find joy in our lives. If that sounds like something you want to be a part of, you're in the right place, and I'm super glad that you're here! Are you ready to change the way you respond to your loved one's addiction problems? I hope so!

How do you feel when you think your daughter's drug addiction is ruining her life?

Hopeless, right? How do you cope with this hopeless feeling? Maybe you don't. You might think, *this isn't really living; I'm dying inside because of her using career.*

What do you have to do to start living for yourself?

Follow me as I take you on the journey where you transform from a seed to a flower. From a mom whose only focus is on her child, to a mom whose focus is on herself.

Using this flower analogy, you will work through seven transformational steps to letting go: Commitment; Self-Awareness; Inner

Dialogue; Creating the Plan; Implementing the Plan; Progress, Reflection, and Vision; Helping Others and Living a New Life.

Once you master this shift in focus, you will help your adult child see that change is possible and that *hope* is the best four-letter word in the dictionary. Children do what children see—no matter how old they are. Once you show your child what hope looks like, your child will see your joy and want what you have.

This book will show you ways to change. There is no magical bullet to help your son or daughter get well. But you can make a difference by your responses to your child's actions. To do this, you must first start with yourself.

I will give you suggestions based on my journey, but it's up to you to act on the information. If my suggestions make you uncomfortable or they don't resonate with you, ponder them for a while. We are all on a different journey and recovery works differently for everyone.

**Don't wait for someone to
bring you flowers. Plant your own garden
and decorate your own soul.**

—Luther Burbank

The Seed: Commitment

Seeds need water, sun, and soil. Seeds are small, but rich with possibility, just like you and your addicted loved one.

If a seed sits in a sealed packet—without nourishment—it won't grow. It will never transform into a beautiful flower. When we don't plant and nourish our seeds, we lose our potency and a powerful symbol of renewal and possibilities.

Growing from the seed stage into a beautiful flower provides hope for the future. Not only for our future, but those around us, including our addicted loved ones (ALOs).

One bright flower in the garden can dominate a whole scene. If the flower stands tall among thorny leaves, it is noticed and appreciated. My hope is that by the end of this guide, you'll have done the work to stand out in the garden of moms who are struggling just like you.

Seeds represent the power of creation—of moms—capable of transforming into something amazing. If we don't plant, water, and fertilize our seeds, we give up on ourselves and our children. When that happens, there's a chance that our seeds won't grow into hopeful stories.

Think of biting into a peach or a strawberry and notice how the juice dribbles down your chin. These luscious sweet fruits started as a seed, but they were nourished and appreciated until they produced fruit you can enjoy.

Your choices dictate whether your seed will flourish or stay in a dark packet and never grow, to never reach a higher potential.

Many moms walk through life paralyzed in uncertainty and fear about their ALO. If you're like me, when I started my journey of recovering as a mom of an addict, I didn't know what to do or what not to do. I couldn't find a support group that could help me find answers.

That's all changed now. Because you're here, you will get the support you need. My guess is that you want to learn since you downloaded this guide. You know if you neglect your seed and don't nurture it, you risk never reaping the reward of a sweet fruit that you want to grow. Many moms get stuck. They don't address their problems or maximize their potential, but you're different because you're here, and I'm thrilled.

I pray that you will find the help you need to grow into a more joy-filled mom. The more moms we have in this movement, the sooner we can stop this addiction cycle.

Michelle Weidenbenner

Print this prayer off below and read it daily to help you on this journey. Or start a recovery journal and write it on the first page.

Mother's Serenity Prayer

**God grant me the ability to surrender my ego
and all forms of control, while understanding I
am powerless over my addict child's behavior, and
give me the wisdom to know that only my addict
child can choose to be drug free, sober, and healthy,
and only when he becomes ready. And so it is.**

Through the process of watching our children lead unhealthy lives, moms are often consumed with worry, anxiety, and fear that they will die. We want to stop that from happening. Isn't it every mother's job to protect her young one?

Yes!

It doesn't matter if they're *adult* children. We will always want to protect them, no matter how old they are. We can't stop wanting to keep them safe. But sometimes our keeping them safe stops them from accepting natural consequences. It's the consequences that help them grow. It's the consequences that bring pain, and no mom wants to see her child in pain. I understand. I've said that my son isn't a criminal. He's sick. I've made all kinds of excuses about him in his lifetime.

Thinking differently about our response to our children takes time. Change is a process. It doesn't happen in a day, but if we work daily on understanding and changing our behavior, the sum of all our efforts will lead to more joy.

BE A SEED THAT GROWS

To begin, tell me what your life is like right now. If you're here, my guess is that you're in pain. What does your life look like now? Are you coping with any of these?

Check all that apply and date the list.

_____ Reduced finances

_____ Worry

_____ Sleeplessness

_____ Consuming thoughts

_____ Shortness of breath

_____ Anger

_____ Eating unhealthy food

_____ Loss of appetite

_____ Separation from spouse

_____ Loss of job

_____ No time for exercise

_____ No church life

_____ No prayer time

_____ Heart racing

_____ Problems parenting
other children

_____ Helplessness

_____ Anxiety or panic

_____ Loss of libido

_____ Weight gain

_____ Reduced personal hygiene

_____ Reactive instead of proactive

_____ Loss of goals or dreams

_____ Hopelessness

_____ Loss of friends

_____ Shame

_____ Regret

_____ Guilt

_____ Others

Date: _____

Michelle Weidenbenner

If you checked any of these above, I'm confident you are not living a joy-filled life. Maybe seeing your check marks on paper will help you visualize your pain.

Below is a happiness scale. To see yourself and gauge your progress, read and complete the scale. This is a safe and simple way to start your recovery. First, you need to see where you are, so you know where you're going to go. When you get in the car to go to the store, you know your destination. It's the same with your goals. If you don't have an end in mind, you'll wander aimlessly. This is a baby step to helping you master and rediscover you.

HAPPINESS SCALE

1. Rate your overall happiness on a scale of 1-10. Ten is the happiest.

_____

_____

_____

_____

2. If you could have one superpower, what would it be and how would you use it?

_____

_____

_____

_____

3. List three things that bring you joy:

_____

_____

_____

_____

4. What situation are you facing right now that you wish you could wake up and find it gone?

_____

_____

_____

_____

5. What are you most thankful for?

_____

_____

_____

_____

6. Name something that makes you unique. Are you proud of it?

_____

_____

_____

_____

7. What is the hardest part of your typical day?

_____

_____

_____

_____

8. What three words do you think most describe you?

_____

_____

_____

_____

9. What are a few of your personal goals that always seem out of reach?

_____

_____

_____

_____

Congratulations!
You planted your seed and are now on your way to germinating!

Plant the seed of positivity into your mind, nourish it daily with love and happiness will flower, as fear begins to die.

—Leon Brown

Germination: Self-Awareness

A seed's first tiny root is called a radicle, which anchors the plant and absorbs water. With this in place, the seed sends a shoot, called a plumule, that eventually sprouts above ground, and the seed becomes a seedling.

You have planted yourself in the richest soil you could find—here in this little guide. You've put out a root that will help anchor you in a supportive environment, and you've sent up a sprout to nourish yourself more.

You are now a seedling.

By completing the Happiness Scale and evaluating your current life status in the last step, you're beginning to grow. You're able to see yourself a little differently.

Let's take a closer look.

A SLAVE TO YOUR ALO

*Slave*ry is defined as a state of being owned by others who control us. No, our children don't own us in the literal sense, but I'm sure their actions have controlled our emotions, actions, lack of sleep, loss of funds, and healthy well-being.

Their addictive choices suck the life out of us. But only because we let them.

Our children's successes and failures are their own. Not ours.

Sometimes, as moms, we want what is best for our children more than they do. When this happens, we cross the line and do something for them that they should do themselves. We think we're helping, but we're not.

When we assume their responsibilities, we create entitlement and dependency in our children rather than empowering them. Don't give in to this temptation.

In his book, *Resisting Happiness*, Matthew Kelly says:

> God has put your child in this world for a specific mission, but first He must prepare him. God wants heaven for your child more than your child wants it for himself. But God doesn't cross the line. He will not step over your child's free will. He wants to empower your child for a mission.

Michelle Weidenbenner

Changing how you respond to your unhealthy child takes *commitment, intentionality,* and *focus*. If you're ready to nourish your roots with fertilizer, here's your first assignment. Executing this step will hold you accountable and encourage you on your journey.

FIGHT FOR YOURSELF FIRST

The first step to becoming a Mighty Mom is to fight for mastery of yourself, instead of behaving like a slave to your ALO. Once you can focus on you, everything changes.

Maybe you've become so disconnected with who you are and what you enjoy doing that you've lost sight of what makes you happy. Hopefully, the happiness scale in the last section showed you that you need a life, so take a deep breath and join a group of moms today!

You need to hang out with people who fit your future, not your history. Addiction thrives in isolation. Recovery thrives in a strong community. Moms will recover.

Go to the FB page: MomsLettingGo (no spaces) and ask to join. Once you're there, share a post or a video post of yourself using this statement:

> My name is (your name). I am a Mighty Mom who wants to ruin my (son/daughter)'s using career, but the only person I can control is myself. Today I'm taking charge of my own life,

so I can find joy. I need support because I want to stop help-ing in the wrong way. Will you help me (specifically list what you want to be accountable for)?

Joining a support group is one of the greatest ways to help yourself. The beauty of this group is that it's online and you don't have to go anywhere. You can pop in and pop out when it's convenient. I call it a peer-group recovery room. It's a wonderful gift to give your child. You'll see why as you grow.

When I first began my journey, I said, "I'm not the problem. My child is the addict. Why do I have to change?"

What I learned was that I was addicted to having obsessive thoughts about my ALO. I couldn't stop ruminating over the negative thoughts in my mind, and they were controlling me. I couldn't let go.

Letting go is a choice, a positive one for you. If you could learn new ways to cope with your child's problem, and new ways to help him, wouldn't you want to do that?

If you could detach from your ALO's poor choices, what would your life look like?

One mother said, "I finally admitted that I couldn't fix my son, so I agreed to let God do it for me." She discovered that love is not a cure for addiction. Love is just a word.

Michelle Weidenbenner

The antidote for addiction is connectivity, but how can moms connect with their ALOs who seem unavailable or appear possessed by a zombie who only wants to kidnap their lives?

You can stay connected to your children through prayers and love. Letting go doesn't mean you abandon them, don't love them, or don't show them compassion. Letting go means that you understand your sense of self and realize that you can't control their actions.

To help with this transition, consider completing the next assignment.

WRITE A *DETACHING* LETTER TO YOUR ALO

Write a letter to your child. In the letter, let him know what you will and won't do going forward. This is a huge step, but one that will help you grow. Whether you send the letter or communicate your thoughts verbally, it is important that your ALO understand these new boundaries.

One letter looked like this:

> **What I won't do**. Your addiction is killing you and it's killing me too. I have to let go of you to save myself. My love for you isn't enough to save you. You must help yourself, love yourself. I'm not a professional, so I can't help you, but you can get professional help if you want to change. You need a solid, dual-diagnosis facility. Until you decide to change, I can't see you. Your emaciated body jolts me into anxiety so deep that

I can't breathe. I will only talk to you by text. If you text me negative and angry messages, I won't answer. If you ask me for food, money, or gas, I will ignore you. (Many moms still feel that buying their ALO a meal is okay. You must decide what's right for you.)

What I will do: I will continue to love you, and I'll shout for God to rebuke Satan in the name of Jesus, so Satan releases his hold on you. I'll pray that one day you'll be strong enough to seek sobriety for good. I will support you in recovery. If you choose to go to a rehab program, I will pray that it's a faith-based program because I believe this is a spiritual journey. I will support your course of treatment.

Every time I saw our son, I struggled to think positive thoughts. I couldn't sleep or eat, so I avoided him. I let my husband take over all communication with him and his wife, so I didn't feel the negative energy that sucked me under. When I didn't see him, I remained calmer, but when I heard an ambulance, I'd fret that maybe he'd died. When I couldn't sleep at night, I was sure that he had overdosed or that he was in trouble.

Yes, I was addicted to having thoughts of him using, and even though I wanted to stop, I couldn't stop ruminating on deadly scenarios.

Michelle Weidenbenner

Below is another example of a letter. My hope is that you find inspiration to write your letter. What I will do and won't do might look different in your letter. The important part of this is to set new boundaries and explain what those will look like for your ALO.

A LETTER TO MY ADULT CHILD ON THE DAY I LET GO WITHOUT GIVING UP

Dear Son,

Today is the day I become a member of a team of moms who want to ruin their children's using career.

I have tried to remove the drug devil from your body in unhealthy ways by making excuses for you, giving you money, providing a safe place for you to stay, and making life easier for you. It hasn't helped you to find a safe, sober, and healthy life. My helping has only delayed the inevitable, delayed the time for you to be accountable for your own actions. The time is now.

We all have our role in your recovery, but who am I to interfere with your journey? Who am I to get in God's way? All I can do is to love you and pray you find your way to a safe, healthy, and sober lifestyle, one that is God's will, one that brings you joy.

This group of moms I belong to is a gift to me. They help me take care of myself, so I can inadvertently give you this gift, the gift of letting go without giving up. I love you and will pray for God to lead you on a journey that will transform your life into something amazing and purposeful. I believe in you. I believe God created you for a purpose, but Satan keeps hijacking your success, so I will cry out to God to rebuke Satan and rid your body from him.

Today you might feel afraid and alone because I won't be there the way I've been. I'm sorry for that, but I'm certain that one day you will thank me for this new plan.

I wish there was a way to do this that was easy, but there isn't. Sometimes doing the right thing is the hardest thing.

Today you will be on your own to figure out how to get well your way. You will meet people who will want to help you on your journey, and people who will use you to get what they want. I pray that you learn to recognize the difference. I can't soften your fall. I wish I could.

Tomorrow you will experience pain, possibly loss of job, arrests, jail time, loss of home, and loss of family if you continue down this destructive path. I pray you don't lose your life.

Today is the day I have to say goodbye to a part of me... and that's you ... when all I want is to hold you and protect you from your actions and consequences. You have many positive memories of us as a family. As you begin your journey, I pray that you will take comfort in some of the good times we've had and know that there are many more awaiting you, but you must get well first.

I can't tell you the best treatment for your illness, but I know there are professionals who can, who care for people who are hurting like you. They help heal others every day, but they only

Michelle Weidenbenner

have the power to help if the patient is willing to undergo the treatment.

Are you strong enough to endure the treatment? Are you ready to try something different? I am.

This won't be easy. If it were easy, then we wouldn't have any addicted loved ones.

You might think that other people don't know you're in active addiction, but they know. You wear it in the way you dress, communicate, and walk across the room. Society's stigma of mental illness and addiction keeps you a prisoner in your own body, unable to admit your pain. Denial keeps you locked in a place where you think, *if I don't admit I have a problem, nobody will ever know, and I won't have to do anything about it.*

If you believe that this is the best way to get well, then who am I to stand in your way?

I must leave you now, not forever, just in the way I've been there for you in the past. There is no way to prepare you for this new journey. You're an adult now, and I'm confident you will figure it out. I did. Your father did. So will you.

Deep inside you is the person I once knew. Even though the drug devil is hiding that person, I saw a glimpse of him today. He is strong. He is beautiful. He is worthy of a purposeful life.

Thank you for allowing me the privilege to serve as your mom for so many years, for trusting me with your most intimate moments. I've been honored to witness these stages in your life.

I will watch from the sidelines and cheer for you to make healthy choices in the next chapters of your life too, to mend from the scars that brought you here, and to see that you are worthy of a joy-filled life.

I pray that you will cheer for me too, as I head out on my journey, as I seek to find joy despite your difficulties. I'm confident that you believe I'm worthy too. If I don't let go, I'll be sucked under with you. The pain of one of my body parts (you) being severed is unbearable. It's easier for me to cope if I don't have to watch it bleed—just like at the doctor's office, I turn away. It will seem like I'm turning away from you too, but I'm not. I'm simply turning my head, so I don't have to see you bleed, watch you suffer.

There is nothing I can do to make your illness go away. Oh, how I wish I could. Please know that I care. We care. The world cares. But behind our worry is a lack of faith, and if we want to start a movement of moms who let go without giving up, we must have faith in your ability, in God's plan for you.

All I can do now is control myself. I must stop trying to control you and tell you what to do. You're old enough to make your own decisions.

Good luck on your journey to becoming the best you that God created you to be.

Love,
Mom

Michelle Weidenbenner

Your mind is a garden.
Your thoughts are the seeds. You can
grow flowers, or you can grow weeds.

—Osho

Breaking Out: Inner Dialogue

The first leaves that appear on a seedling are called seed leaves. They are part of the seed's embryo and provide nutrients until the true leaves appear. The moms you've reached out to have helped you grow stronger, similar to the seed leaves. You aren't alone. You surrounded yourself with necessary nutrients and found power in sharing.

The true leaves that form from the embryo turn energy from sunlight, water, and carbon dioxide into sugars, which the plant uses for food.

Your mind can do the same for you.

If you nourish your brain by providing sunlight (an awareness), fertilizer (prayers and support) and water (learning new ways to cope), you will develop energy called Mighty Mom Power. What you say to yourself, your inner dialogue, has the potential to ramp up the mom superpower. It all begins and ends with you and your thoughts.

What thoughts are you giving power to today? Whatever you give power to ... has power over you.

Your mind grows as you take the energy of positive thinking and support groups and use them for food. By listening and changing your inner dialogue, you have the power to nourish your soul and change the trajectory of your happiness and daily output.

First, you must identify the lies you've believed about yourself and your abilities. Then you must develop positive self-talk that gives you the capacity to harvest more nutrients or attract other positive people and their support.

As the plant grows upward and forms new leaves at the top of the stem, it grows downward, too, growing more roots. This growth helps the plant to soak in more water and nutrients, which helps it withstand weather, animal disturbances, and competition from other plants.

When you develop more positive self-talk, you're able to see the possibilities around you, which will give you more energy and help you become more resilient, confident, and surer of yourself. You will be able to weather your ALO's negative comments or poor choices more effectively too.

What are the lies you tell yourself? Check those that apply.

____ I'm not good at math.

____ I caused my child's problem.

____ I am weak.

____ More money will solve my problems.

____ I can never say no.

____ I don't have enough time.

____ I'm not good at _____. I could never learn.

____ I'm too old.

____ I'm too young.

____ I'll do it when I have the time.

____ I'm ugly.

____ I'm stupid.

____ I'm too impatient.

____ I need to go to college first.

____ I don't know where to start.

____ I can't do anything about it.

____ I'm not ready.

____ I don't know what to do.

____ If I could just _____, my life would be amazing.

____ No one understands me.

____ I have a mental block.

____ I'm a failure.

____ I can't hold a job.

____ If my son/daughter would get sober, all my problems would be over.

____ If I had the money to move away, everything would be better.

____ I'm a terrible parent.

____ Others—you name them. Identify them.

Date: _____

Write every lie below so you can stare it in the face. Confront it. Don't believe the lies that you tell yourself when you're losing hope. Lies steal your happiness. You can do something about your life, and I know you're ready because you've made it this far.

_____

_____

_____

_____

_____

_____

_____

_____

POSITIVE SELF-TALK

Positive self-talk builds resilience and makes us better Mighty Moms. But where do we start? How do we find and build this superpower?

1. Start a gratitude wall or journal. Every day, write one positive thing on a sticky note or in a journal, even if it's something as simple as "my coffee was hot today." This will help you see the positive events in your day.

Michelle Weidenbenner

2. Recite these during tense moments:

- I can do something about this.
- Life is a beautiful challenge.
- I am ready.
- I am a Mighty Mom.
- My life is amazing.
- I am not my failures.
- All the answers lie within me.
- There are people who understand and support me.

"If your heart is broken, make art with the pieces."
—Shane Koyczan

3. Practice self-compassion. Have you ever watched a dog's behavior toward its owner? Dogs know how to comfort: they listen, console, never interrupt, and they forgive us quickly. We could learn from dogs by treating ourselves the same way.

Living with an addicted child is traumatizing.

Every day we're faced with uncertainty and disruption because of their choices. Typically, as moms, we take care of ourselves last, but we need to change that. The flight attendant on a plane tells you to put your mask on first—before your child's. Our children take our lead, and if we're not good to ourselves or don't take care of ourselves, they see it and think we must not be worth it. They walk all over us without batting an eyelash.

You are worth it!

There are ways we can catch ourselves lacking self-compassion. Listen for the signs below.

When you say or think:

- I'm stressed.
- This sucks.
- I don't have a minute to myself.
- I can't hear myself think.

When you can't get those thoughts out of your head, there's a good chance that you aren't showing your ALO healthy limits or boundaries, and it's stomping on your self-love. Something or someone (or both) are stopping you from a healthy mindset.

What can you do about it?

1. Journal your feelings without holding back so you recognize exactly what triggers you to feel this way. Become aware of the cause. Awareness is key. If we don't notice patterns, we can't change them.

_____

_____

_____

_____

_____

_____

_____

2. Share your frustrations in a support group where others understand. When you realize you're not alone, you have hope.

3. Place your hand on your heart or hold your hand up and repeat a mantra similar to this: "Take time for yourself today, Michelle. You're worth it. Give yourself grace. You aren't perfect. You are worthy of God's love. You are His daughter."

4. Think how you would treat a friend if she were going through the same thing you are. What would you say? *I'm sorry. I'll pray for you. I'm here if you need to talk.*

5. Write a letter to yourself. (Or type one. This works better for me.) Maybe you can audio-text the letter to yourself. Label it a self-compassion letter. Set aside just ten minutes. It might look something like this:

> Dear Mighty Mom,
>
> You are doing the best you can do given your situation. You're not perfect. Yes, you're ashamed of how you handled your ALO today. (Or insert something else.) You'll try better next time. Invite God into your life, so you feel support, so you feel stronger. Faith is the opposite of worry.
>
> Everyone has difficulties in their lives. You're no exception. Who are you to think you should be excluded? Embrace what you have. Let your family love you. Accept their love with open arms. See the goodness and the kindness of those around you. Be kind to yourself. Love yourself. You matter. Your life matters. Find ways to serve others, and you will reap the reward."
> Sign it. Date it.

Your letter:

_____

_____

_____

_____

_____

_____

_____

_____

_____

_____

_____

_____

What does your letter look like? Are you bold enough to share it on our Facebook page (MomsLettingGo)? Post it there. I dare you. I double dare you.

When you share your struggles with others who, like you, don't see the value in themselves or take the time to notice, you will not only encourage them but also encourage yourself.

WHOSE ADDICTION IS IT?

Stop for a minute and think about this ... what if you're addicted to thinking, obsessing, and worrying about your ALO? Is that possible?

I was addicted.

You think your ALO's addiction problem is his, and you want to help him, but maybe you need to think differently. What if you have an addiction? I know it sounds crazy, and I don't want to offend you, but I do want to help you.

In her book, *Loving What Is: Four Questions That Can Change Your Life*, Byron Katie says, "A thought is harmless unless we believe it. It's not our thoughts, but the attachment to our thoughts that causes suffering. Attaching to a thought means believing that it's true, without inquiring. A belief is a thought that we've been attaching to, often for years" (page 5).

CONSIDER YOUR THOUGHTS

Do they play like a movie over and over in your head? Maybe your thoughts sound a little like some of mine have:

- He will overdose and die if I don't help him to see what he's doing.
- If I buy him a place to stay maybe he'll be able to cope better and feel better, so he'll stop using.
- Maybe if I buy him a car to get around, he'll have more opportunities to get a better job.
- Maybe if I let him stay here and live with me, he can get on his feet and eventually be living on his own.
- Maybe if I take care of his kids for a while, he'll be able to get on his feet.
- If I don't take care of my grandkids, their lives will be in danger.
- He just had a bad day. Tomorrow will be better.

Michelle Weidenbenner

A lot of pain you're dealing with stems from your thoughts. They are only thoughts.

If you look deeply at each one of your thoughts and ask, can I prove that this is true? You might be surprised to find that no, your thoughts can't be proven true. When you realize your thoughts might not be true, why give them power? If you take control of your thoughts, you can find peace.

I recommend reading Byron Katie's book, *Loving What Is: Four Questions That Can Change Your Life*. (You can go to www.thework. com to learn more and find other helpful tools.) Her four questions, referred to as "The Work," are easy to implement and will teach you to turn your thoughts around. And if you can turn your thoughts around, you will lead a more joy-filled life. I promise.

Here are her four questions:

- Is it true?
- Can you absolutely know that it's true?
- How do you react, what happens, when you believe that thought?
- Who would you be without the thought?

Now let's complete a two-part exercise, and at the end we'll apply the four questions to a sample response.

Part 1. Identify the thoughts that are causing your stress and write them down:

_____

_____

_____

_____

_____

_____

_____

_____

Don't hold back. No one is going to read this or judge you. Use short, simple sentences. You don't have to spell or punctuate properly. Write how your ALO is causing you stress. Don't be tempted to do this in your head instead of writing it down. Sit with paper and pen and let the words spill on the page. There's power in seeing your words on paper. Trust me on this.

When your son or daughter is in active addiction and you're sitting on the sidelines watching, you can be frightened out of your mind and lost inside your mind's chaos. But when you enter *the work* zone, it's possible to find order and peace. You will learn how to find your way back home.

Michelle Weidenbenner

Katie says, "When you do *the work*, you see who you are by seeing who you think other people are. Eventually you come to see that everything outside you reflects your own thinking. You are the storyteller, the projector of all stories, and the world is the projected image of your thoughts" (Page 12).

Instead of trying to change your ALO, you must look inward to how you can change yourself, and in this case, it starts with your thoughts. Learn to change the direction of your thoughts, and you can find peace.

Part 2. Considering all the thoughts and stressors you identified in Part 1, complete the following:

A. List how your ALO angers, confuses, saddens, or disappoints you and why. Write what upsets you the most about the situation.

_____

_____

_____

_____

_____

_____

_____

_____

B. How do you want this person to change? What do you want him/her to do? If you were this person, how would you want you to change? List what you want him/her to do no matter how childish your wants are.

_____

_____

_____

_____

_____

_____

_____

_____

C. What advice would you offer her/him? Make your advice specific, practical, and detailed. Articulate the steps how he should carry out your advice. Would this advice solve your problem in A above?

_____

_____

_____

_____

_____

_____

_____

_____

D. For you to be happy in this situation, what do you need your ALO to think, say, feel, or do? If your ALO took your advice, would that take you all the way to your happy place and stop your pain?

_____

_____

_____

_____

_____

_____

_____

_____

E. What do you think of your ALO in this situation? Make a list. (Feel free to be petty and judgmental.)

_____

_____

_____

_____

_____

_____

_____

_____

F. What is it about this situation that you don't want to experience again?

_____

_____

_____

_____

_____

_____

_____

Now let's use Katie's "The Work" questions to evaluate one of the most common thoughts moms of ALOs have: *my son/daughter will die from this disease.*

Question 1: Is it true? *Yes, it seems that way. People are dying every day from overdoses.*

Question 2: Can you absolutely know that it's true? *No, because there are others who recover and live a sober life.*

Question 3: How do you react, what happens, when you believe that specific thought? *When I believe that my child will die, I can't breathe. I think ... I must save him. Now! There must be something I can do.*

Michelle Weidenbenner

Question 4: Who would you be without this thought? *Oh, my. If I didn't have this thought controlling my life, I could breathe and sleep and smile.*

Apply these questions to some of your responses in the exercise. I didn't describe *the work* the in-depth way Byron Katie does in her book, but if this process intrigues you like it did me, please consider reading her book.

No one is responsible for your suffering except you. If you think that something or someone is the cause for your problems, your situation will feel hopeless You will be in a *victim* situation. But when you bring truth to the forefront, like I did in the example exercise above, you will begin to set yourself free.

How are you showing yourself compassion when you play the video in your head repeatedly with a thought that torments you? You aren't. You replay this video because you can't control your own thinking. Many of us aren't even aware of our obsessive thoughts.

I'm not a mind reader. Are you? Yet we often think we know what someone else is thinking, especially when it's negative about us. All we can do is turn our thoughts around; it's our thoughts, versus facts, that are the source of much of our stress.

Our thoughts are often the reason we aren't coping well. Once those negative thoughts are brought into the open, we can analyze them to determine if they are true.

If you want to break out and take control of your life, keep going and reach up to the next chapter.

Michelle Weidenbenner

Flowers do not bloom without a little rain.
Everything has its purpose, even pain.

—Averstu.com

Reaching Up for a New Leaf on Life: Creating the Plan

O nce a plant begins to grow, the stem reaches up and follows the sunlight. Parenchyma cells are the most common plant cells found in the stem, the leaf, and the pulp of the fruit. Parenchyma cells are responsible for metabolic functions, such as photosynthesis, and they help repair and heal wounds.

As your hope for your own health grows stronger, so will your hope for your ALO. Your new mindset will grow *cells* like the parenchyma. They will help you begin to heal and understand your ALO with deeper clarity.

There's a greater chance that your flower will bloom, that you will achieve more joy in your life, because now you're taller and better anchored in the ground. You've surrounded yourself in a nurturing environment, you've taken control of your thoughts, so like the stem of this plant, your confidence will rise too.

You'll continue to reach up and search God's purpose for you. I hope that you are beginning to see that you have a new *leaf on life*!

"Unless commitment is made, there are only promises and hopes, but no plans."
—Peter F. Drucker

If I could wave a magic wand that would give you a new life, what would that look like? How would your life change? If you're like most moms of an addict, you would want a sober son or daughter, one who was employed, independent, and secure in his or her life, with a strong faith in God. Can you see this or dream it?

In this exercise, be honest about your hopes and dreams. Write what your life would look like if you got your wish, if your son or daughter was healthy:

Michelle Weidenbenner

What are your five most important core values?

A list is included below to get you started. There are no right or wrong answers. Your core values reflect your priorities and are part of your unique self. Choosing only five might be difficult for you. If that's the case, feel free to list more. See if you can number them in importance. Try not to rush. Highlight which ones matter the most to you.

Examples include:

appearance	education	loyalty
appreciation	efficiency	motivation
assertiveness	environmentalism	open-mindedness
cleanliness	faith	optimism
commitment	fitness	passion
communication	flexibility	patriotism
compassion	focus	perseverance
confidence	good humor	positivity
consistency	gratitude	reliability
courage	growth	respect
creativity	honesty	sacrifice
curiosity	innovation	service to others
dependability	integrity	spirituality
education	loyalty	tithing

List Your Core Values Below

Are your core values in line with what you're living with to-day? If not, look to God for answers.

THE PLAN

"If you fail to plan,
you are planning to fail."
—Benjamin Franklin.

First you had to become aware of the need for change. Nothing changes if nothing changes, and you realized that you're the only person you can change. Then you found ways to surround yourself with support. Next you identified ways to improve your inner dialogue. Now it's time to discover exactly what you want.

The exercises above should have helped you define what you want, and how you want your life to look. Now it's time to create your plan. Below is a worksheet you can complete to get started.

MOMS LETTING GO WORKSHEET

Your Action Plan to Become a Joy-Filled Mom

What do you want? Write everything that comes to mind.

_____

_____

_____

_____

_____

_____

What are you not doing that you wish you had more time to do?

_____

_____

_____

_____

_____

_____

What social events will you add to your life?

_____

_____

_____

_____

_____

_____

What spiritual actions will you add to your life?

_____

_____

_____

_____

_____

What volunteer or vocational actions will you add to your life?

_____

_____

_____

_____

_____

What physical actions will you take:

_____

_____

What are the consequences if you don't follow through with your action plan?

_____

_____

_____

_____

_____

How will you track your progress?

_____

_____

_____

_____

_____

Michelle Weidenbenner

Which habits do you want to replace? List them.

_____

_____

_____

_____

_____

_____

_____

_____

When will you start?

_____

_____

_____

How often will you review your progress?

_____

_____

_____

_____

What rewards will you add to applaud your efforts?

_____

_____

_____

_____

_____

_____

Who will hold you accountable?

_____

_____

_____

_____

_____

_____

_____   _____

Date   Signature

_____   _____

Date   Friend/Accountability Partner Signature

Please share a part of your plan with us at the FB page, so we can encourage you and be inspired by your progress.

Here's an example of what a plan might look like.

What do you want?

To replace worry with joy despite my ALO's choices.

Worry and fear have caused me to neglect my self-care, so I will make time for my own health. Worrying has caused me to overeat, lose sleep, gain weight, and neglect my family and friends. Even when I feel like it's wrong, I'll go through the motions of doing what pleases me instead of taking care of my ALO. Hopefully, in time, I will automatically choose me.

What are you not doing that you wish you had more time for?

Exercise, crafts, pickleball, baking, sewing, attending leadership seminars, going on vacation with my husband, having date nights with my husband, spending time with my other children and my girlfriends, going to church, attending support group meetings, writing.

What social events will you add to your life?

Join a book group, go out with my girlfriends once a month, meet for dinner with my husband and another couple once a month. Plan an annual vacation with my husband.

What spiritual actions will you add to your life:

Attend church once a week. Spend fifteen minutes every morning reading devotionals that focus on my recovery. I will start a gratitude journal and write something each day that I'm thankful for. If I get stuck and revert back to old habits, I'll seek a counselor. I'll join a local support group. We have a PAL group in our city. (Parents of Addicted Loved Ones) I'll attend that twice a month.

What volunteer or vocational actions will you add to your life:

I will volunteer once a month in the nursery at church because I love toddlers.

What physical actions will you take:

I will play pickleball twice a week. I will walk three days a week for a minimum of a half hour. I will park farther away, so I have to walk more.

How will you track your progress?

I will use Google Forms to create my own chart, put it on the refrigerator and check off those things I do for myself to help build a healthier me. If I struggle with creating my own form, I'll search Google for a free form that I can print and use.

Michelle Weidenbenner

Which habits do you want to replace? What will you replace them with?

Instead of watching two hours of TV at night, I'll read for an hour, then I'll walk for a half hour or play cards with my husband (depending on the weather), and I'll journal for another half hour.

Instead of complaining, I will write positive affirmations to myself in my journal or add to my gratitude journal.

When I feel myself worrying about something that I have no control over, I'll read devotionals or Bible verses, call my accountability partner, or listen to Christian music. I'll have to assess which one works best.

I won't look at my phone every other minute, waiting for my ALO to text me. Instead, I will leave my phone in another room and only check it once every hour. To stop waking up during the night to check my phone, I will turn it off. When my ALO texts me hate notes, I will not reply. Instead, I will say to myself, *this is not my child. I refuse to respond to the devil who has possessed his soul.*

When my ALO has a problem and wants me to solve it for him, I'll empower him to find his own solutions by saying, "I'm confident that you will figure it out."

When will you start?

Tomorrow.

How often will you review your progress?

The first Tuesday of each month I will assess my progress and make adjustments. I will celebrate my wins and see where I'm falling short and adjust. I will give myself grace if I don't follow through with my plan, but if I see a pattern where I'm weak, I will bring it up in support group or with my counselor to work through.

What are the consequences if you don't follow through with your action plan?

If I don't take control of my life, I'll never find joy. I'll fall back into the unhealthy habits and put everyone else before me. I will continue to gain weight, which will increase my glucose levels. My blood pressure could accelerate if I don't change what I'm doing too.

What rewards will you add to applaud your efforts?

- I'll share my progress with the FB group, friends who under-stand, and my husband because those people will compliment me on my progress.
- When I lose five pounds, I'll buy a smaller outfit.
- When my blood pressure is down for an entire week, I'll treat myself to a manicure.

Michelle Weidenbenner

- When I don't take responsibility for my ALO's choices by empowering him to manage them himself, I'll treat myself to a healthy snack or a skinny latte at Starbucks.

Who will hold you accountable?

My friend Barb is struggling with an addicted adult child. She understands what I'm going through. I will ask her if she'll be my accountability partner. If she isn't interested, I'll reach out to a mom at the MomsLettingGo FB page and find someone who wants to join me on this recovery journey.

Other parts of your plan might include:

I will:

- Pay attention to my inner dialogue.
- Only speak nice thoughts to myself.
- Give myself grace.
- Not take responsibility for anyone but myself.
- Admit that I've been addicted to helping him/her.
- Quit blaming my quality of life on my ALO.
- Stop saying, "When my ALO gets into rehab/recovery, I will get my life back."
- Take charge of my life now while I still have a life.
- Decide who and what I will allow into my life.
- Set limits and boundaries that I'm comfortable with.
- Stop negative self-talk.

- Love my ALO no matter what.
- Accept my ALO for the life he chooses, even if I don't agree with the choices.
- Make choices only for me and no one else.

As you're writing your plan, ask yourself: Does this support the life I'm working to create for myself? Does this support my values that I listed above?

Why not write this statement (below) in your journal? Date it and sign it. When you're overwhelmed with grief over your ALO's choices, reread your statement:

I choose to separate my life from my ALO's. I'm not giving up. I'm surrendering my life to God, and I know that I can't control anyone but myself. I'm not responsible for my ALO's happiness or his problems. He owns his own life, and who am I to get in the way of his journey?

Let's head over to the **strengthening** part of this guide, to immerse ourselves deeper into the multilayered pieces of the plan.

Where flowers bloom, so does hope.

—Lady Bird Johnson

Strengthening:
Implementing the Plan

*O*nce upon a time, I was a regular mom, stumbling through parent-hood like everyone else — and then I had to figure out how to be the mom of an addict.

I had to figure out how to love my child without helping to hurt him, how to grieve the loss of my child who was still alive (without dying), and how to trade shame and blame for strength.

To be the mom of an addict is to be an ambassador of truth and understanding.

No more shame. No more silence.

—Sandy Swenson, author of *The Joey Song*

"A goal without a plan is just a wish."
—Antoine de Saint-Exupery

As a flower continues to grow, its roots spread deeper and wider, **strengthening** its leaves and its chances of survival. Without continued nurturing, it won't get to the budding stage. If you've ever had a flower garden, you know that there are a lot of factors that contribute to its success. We want more than leaves in our garden, so we need a plan. Do our flowers need sun or shade? How much water do they need? Should we plant them in peat moss or Miracle Grow soil? If we want our plants to bloom, we must plant them in the healthiest environment, water them, and fertilize them.

The same is true of our interactions with our ALOs. If we want to grow and change the way we respond to our children, we need to implement our plans from the last chapter, so we have the best chance at success. Growing means developing new healthy habits, but this takes time.

Recovery is a process, not an event. We can't change the way we react to our ALOs in a day. But we can change over time if we're intentional and committed.

Calculus takes six months to two years to understand. A bachelor's degree typically takes four years.

When I quit smoking thirty-seven years ago, it was tough. I substituted pretzels for cigarettes. I sucked on the pretzel sticks and held them between my fingers, just to hold something that resembled a cigarette. It worked for me, and I quit cold turkey. However, this was a habit that had clear boundaries. If I was going to quit, I had to never smoke another cigarette.

It isn't as clear-cut to quit helping our ALOs, and rarely happens in cold turkey fashion. My hope for you is that you can quit unhealthy helping on your own time. It probably won't be cold turkey, because it's super difficult to know which is the right way and the wrong way to help. It's personal, and nobody can tell you what to do or not do.

If you want to implement your plan for healthy helping, the boundaries might look different depending on where you are in the recovery process. What you're willing to let go of today, might not be what you'll be willing to let go of six months from now. You might only agree to take baby steps because you aren't able to let go of everything yet.

Sometimes if we find healthy substitutions, we can develop new habits, which will help, but first we must find a plan and surround ourselves with support systems.

To help you understand what healthy helping looks like, here are two short lists of unhealthy versus healthy helping behaviors. Surrounding yourself with support will help you make the healthy-helping choices. There are many other moms who are working on their own recovery, just like you. Find them and build accountability partners. Go to the Facebook (FB) page MomsLettingGo and search for someone who is working toward the same goals.

Check which one of the following apply to you. Feel free to add others that you struggle with.

Examples of unhealthy helping:

- Lying to others and yourself about your ALO's behavior.
- Putting the addict's needs before your own.
- Bailing the addict out of messes he/she has created.
- Giving the addict money.
- "Parenting" the addict and feeling resentful about it because he or she is old enough to know better.
- Doing things for the addict that he or she should be doing themselves (taking care of chores, bills, their children).
- _____

Examples of healthy helping:

- Admitting to yourself that the addiction won't go away on its own.
- Putting your needs first—getting support.
- Letting the addict experience consequences for his/her behavior.
- Giving the addict love, not money.
- Setting healthy boundaries for yourself.
- Giving the addict space to take control of his or her own life.

The substitution list seems simple, but when we implement our boundaries and switch one habit for another, we find that it's not easy.

Michelle Weidenbenner

Our "mom" emotions get in the way of common sense. If you're like me, you've helped in some bizarre ways.

If our addict was someone else's child, we would recognize unhealthy helping right away, but because we've raised this child and love him, our emotions hijack our common sense. We want our child to have the life we envisioned him to have. We want him to get well, so we try and make things easier for him, so he finds success.

Do you remember a time when you wanted something so badly that you were willing to do the grueling work to achieve this? When I was fifteen, I wanted contact lenses. I had thick glasses and was self-conscious. I babysat hours and hours so I could afford to buy lenses. I saved $500, which is what they cost in 1972. That was a lot of money, but I was determined to look better and feel better. My parents didn't pay for them. The lenses weren't a need because my parents had already bought me glasses. These were a want, which meant I had to pay for them myself.

What have you done that took true grit? My guess is that you've done, and still do, many things. Your child can too, but first you must empower him, help him to see that he is capable.

His emotional age may be much younger than he truly is, but if you start treating him like his chronological age and giving him age-appropriate responsibilities, perhaps his emotional age will catch up to his true age.

However, for your child to be motivated to change, you must let him experience pain that is far worse than the pleasure he's getting from using a substance. If you keep making life easier on him, you're making your own life chaotic, and not taking care of yourself.

Does that make sense?

If we keep rescuing our loved ones, we get in God's way. It's pride that makes us think we can do what only God can do. We are not our children's Holy Spirit.

Here's a way to allow natural consequences to motivate your ALO. This might help you figure out what you're willing to give up so you can let go and let God and nature take over. (This was inspired by the book, *Beyond Addiction, How Science and Kindness Help People Change*, by Jeffrey Foote, PHD, Carrie Wilkens, PHD, and Nicole Kosanke, PHD, with Stephanie Higgs. This is another book I recommend.)

1. What are you struggling with? (List them.) Examples include:

- Driving him and picking him up when he's not sober.
- Paying his bills or giving him money.
- Watching his children when he is too compromised.
- Bailing him out of jail or protecting him from natural legal consequences.
- Calling into work for him.
- Making excuses for his behavior.
- Taking care of his needs when he's hungover.

2. Brainstorm how you could change your behavior. Put every step on the page. Don't eliminate any ideas. Examples might be not answering her texts when they're belligerent, or calling in sick for her, or taking care of her children so she can party, etc.

_____

_____

_____

_____

_____

_____

3. Cross out those ideas you can't live with. Safety was a huge factor for me when letting go.

When my grandchildren were young, I used to give them sleep-overs at Mimi's house, but each time I did, their parents would party. By taking away the parents' responsibility for their children, I allowed Mom and Dad to use without painful consequences.

The problem was that I feared what would happen if their parents partied while the girls were present. I suspected that their mom was locking the oldest in her bedroom, but I couldn't prove it. My traumatized granddaughter told me what had happened. When I approached my son about the issue, he told me that his child was lying. She was three. I highly doubted she was lying, especially after she would cry hysterically when she was in a room and thought she couldn't get out.

But I couldn't convince my son that there was a problem, so anytime I could babysit and offer a safe environment for the kids, I did. Was that the right way to handle it? There's no clear answer. One might say that I enabled the children's parents, but at that time in my "recovery" I wasn't able to look the other way.

There were several times in our grandchildren's lives that Child Protective Services (CPS) was called, but because there had never been reports of physical abuse, CPS didn't intervene. After our son's arrest for meth possession, CPS came to talk to the girls at school and visit their house. My daughter-in-law coached the oldest child on what to say and how to lie. Therefore, CPS never intervened.

There were some things I couldn't let go of, and I'm sure I helped in the wrong ways many times, but I didn't care. You will feel the same. Only you can make the decision on what you're comfortable doing or not doing.

However, keep in mind that the pain of our ALO's consequences needs to be more than the pleasure for them to want to change.

4. Tell your ALO what your new plan is. State what you will and won't do going forward. Communicate your plan with your spouse and significant others who need to support you before you approach your ALO. They might have valuable input. Feel free to share your plan on our private Facebook group. Many other moms will gain courage from reading your plan. You'll inspire them and possibly gain insight from them. Next, choose a time to talk to your ALO when you're calm and your ALO is mellow. Try not to express your new plans while you're in a fit of anger. Since you're in the strengthening part of your journey, you will build muscle memory and accountability for yourself too.

5. Follow through. Once you've implemented your plan, get out of your child's way, and keep your distance from your ALO if it helps you follow through. When something happens to your ALO, implement your plan. Remind him in a calm and loving way that you're not going to help in this way. Tell him you're confident that he'll figure it out. Tell him you love him.

6. Expect harsh ramifications. Your ALO might swear at you, hang up on you, call you names and tell you that he's going to kill himself. If he's threatened suicide before and gotten your attention, he might try it again. In my opinion, this kind of threat must be taken seriously.

You must decide what you will and won't do. According to a 2014 blog post, "Suicide: One of Addiction's Hidden Risks," by Carolyn C. Ross, M.D., M.P.H, on *Psychology Today's* website, people with substance abuse disorders are about six times more likely to commit suicide than the general population. Suicide threats aren't something to take lightly.

If my child threatens suicide, I will do everything in my power to keep him alive. But I also know that I'm not in control. If he dies, it's not my fault, but that won't comfort me.

Obviously, you don't want to lose your child, and as mom you will do what you think is right to keep your child alive. But ask yourself this ... can you prevent him from dying in a car accident every time he gets behind the wheel? Can you prevent him from contracting a terminal disease? Can you control his life?

After you implement your plan, your child might struggle with the changes you make. If you can connect with your child and can interact in a calm and loving way, below is an example of how you might show empathy and compassion about how he or she is dealing with this transition.

EXERCISE TO SHOW EMPATHY AND COMPASSION

Choose a time when you're calm and when your child is relatively alert. Put away all cell phones and other social media devices so your ALO knows he has your full attention. Ask him if there was something on his mind that's been bothering him. Or if there is something he'd like to talk about.

1. Take time to listen.
2. Focus on him, not on what you will do to help him or rescue him, but on his feelings. Try not to think about what you're going to say next.
3. Be a mirror—repeat what he says. Rephrase his words.
4. Empathize. Let him hear your understanding words.
5. Give him a hug.
6. Tell him you're sorry he's struggling.

7. Let him know that you're confident he will figure out a solution to his problem. (Even if you have no clue as to how he will overcome his challenges.)
8. Say, "I love you."
9. Walk away.

Example dialogue might look like this:

"Is there something troubling you, Jake?" Mom asks her son.

"Yes. I lost my job."

"Oh. I'm sorry. Come and sit down." Mom motions to the kitchen table. She puts her cell phone aside and looks him in the eye. She doesn't react about his losing his job. She remains calm. (Even though inside she wants to shout, quit using drugs!)

Her son sits across from her at the table. "My boss is a jerk. I came in late twice and now I'm out." He bangs the table with his fist.

"I'm sorry. It sounds like you thought you'd have more chances. Rejection hurts."

"I don't know how I'm going to pay rent. My cell phone bill is due too."

Mom gives his arm a love pat. "Owing people money is tough. I'm confident you'll get another job or find a way to pay your bills. Would you like me to pray for you?"

Son jerks his arm out of her hold. "No, I want you to fork over some cash. I have bills to pay. I'm going to be kicked out of my house."

On the inside, Mom is screaming, *no*, because she doesn't want him moving back in with her. They tried that before, and it didn't work. "I'm sorry you're struggling, but I'm sure something will come along."

"So, you're not going to help me?"

Mom shakes her head. "I'm helping you by giving you a chance to stand on your own two feet. Giving you money isn't going to solve your problems. But I love you, and I believe in you."

Son storms out the front door and lets it slam behind him.

***

Mom sits at the kitchen table, weak and trembling. She hates this, but she's proud of herself because she's been working on setting limits and she already identified what she will and won't do. In the past, she gave him money. She'd had that meeting with him and told him she wouldn't help him pay his bills anymore. She must stick to her plan now. She knows that he will call her and text her with belligerent remarks, but she's going to call a friend that she met in support group, so she has accountability and stays strong.

Right now, she feels like calling her son and giving him more money. But instead, she calls her support partner.

If her son calls, she has a plan. She won't respond to negative comments. She knows she's doing the right thing, but it feels awful. She also knows that until she does this a few times, it won't feel natural or sincere because she's never done this before.

She's confident he'll end up in jail, but she can't do anything about it. She gets out a devotional (or Bible) and prays.

Now it's your turn. Write a realistic dialogue that will help you stay focused. Seeing it in your mind will help you play it out in real life.

_____

_____

_____

_____

_____

_____

_____

_____

_____

_____

_____

_____

Be sure to share your experience with our Facebook team. We want to hear your wins and cheer for you! Even if it doesn't go as well as you wanted, having support can help you the next time.

In order to bloom, you must grow.

—Aly Aubrey

Budding: Progress, Reflection, and Vision

This is where the colorful beauty begins. We can finally see the promise of something brighter, bigger, and bolder. We recognize the most visual change in the flower at this stage because of the contrast in color and texture between the petals and the leaves. We anticipate what the full flower will look like, and we notice the progress of all our efforts. The bud is like a new life, full of promise.

You are in the budding stages of a recovering mom. As you grow and learn, you begin to unfurl too. A bud, starting small and simple, then increasing in breadth, complexity, and beauty as you pursue and increase your potential. You show promise to do great things. This is when your friends and family and ALO might notice you shining a little brighter.

When a flower is a bud, it's surrounded by sepals. They protect the flower bud and are behind or underneath the petals when the flower opens.

Now that you're at this stage of developing as a mom, you should be surrounded by other moms who are like these sepals, who are there to cover your back when you finally bloom, to guide you until you're finally able to break out of your old habits and embrace your new ones.

When you don't see progress for your efforts, you lose the fight. You give up. You relapse, just like your ALO. You want to look in the mirror and see the contrast in yourself, but how can you see your progress if it's minuscule? Progress is difficult to measure, especially if you're living in chaos and dysfunction, and a life that's so busy you can't make time for yourself.

Often progress is like doing the cha-cha. There are nine steps in the cha-cha dance, and it isn't until the seventh step that you move forward, or bud. Progress is slow. It will happen, but you must commit to intentionality and consistency every day.

If you're not tracking where you were and comparing it with where you are now, how will you measure where you've been? You'll miss the transition. Go back and read your journal notes from a week ago, a month ago. How long ago did you start your recovery journey? Read all the way back to the beginning. How have you grown? Keep a chart or a spread sheet, or a file with notes and your plan, so you can watch your progress.

Experience isn't the best teacher. It's reflective experience that helps us see our progress. When we can look back and evaluate and reflect what we've been through, we can see what's worked and what hasn't worked.

Below is a list of questions you can use to reflect on your experiences. Look it over once every two weeks, or once a month, but take time to notice your budding self.

Track Your Progress   **Date**_____

How much time has lapsed since you planted your seed?

_____

_____

_____

_____

What's happened in your garden?

_____

_____

_____

_____

Reflect on what you've done to help your ALO and what you haven't done.

_____

_____

_____

_____

Compare what you said you would do with what you said you wouldn't.

_____

_____

_____

_____

Are you growing as strong as you hoped?

_____

_____

_____

_____

What could help you find more joy?

_____

_____

_____

_____

Who could you surround yourself with that would hold you accountable?

_____

_____

_____

_____

Who could help encourage you on your journey?

_____

_____

_____

_____

If you don't document where you were and where you are now, you won't see your progress. In the same way, if you don't have a map to where you're going, how will you know if you've arrived?

What do you have to lose if you don't follow your plan for joy? What will the consequences be for each of these aspects of your life?

1. Your finances

_____

_____

_____

_____

_____

_____

2. Your stress

_____

_____

_____

_____

_____

_____

3. Your health

_____

_____

_____

_____

_____

_____

4. Your child

_____

_____

_____

Michelle Weidenbenner

_____

_____

_____

5. Your spouse

_____

_____

_____

_____

_____

_____

6. Your job

_____

_____

_____

_____

_____

_____

7. Your friends

_____

_____

_____

_____

_____

_____

Identify Problems you have with shifting from one way of helping to the new way. Mark all that apply.

I have trouble with:

_____Following through, especially when my ALO is angry or I feel like I'm pushing him away.

_____Finding strength to follow through with planned consequences.

_____Trusting God that He will guide me and my child.

_____Asking other Moms of Addicts for help because I don't want to hear what they have to say.

_____Worrying that my child is hungry and alone.

_____Anxious about whether my child will die because of my boundaries.

_____Others— list them:

_____

_____

_____

Michelle Weidenbenner

What is your vision for your new life free of your ALO's choices?

If you had more time for you, what would you do? What would your day look like? Where would you find joy? Some of this might seem redundant but where you are today is different from yesterday.

List anything and everything, so you have something to measure later. Are there parts of your life that you've put on hold until your child is well? If you could wave a magic wand and make your child well, how would you spend your time? What are those fun things you used to do for yourself that you have forgotten about? (Writing, knitting, walking the beach, playing cards, visiting the elderly, bowling, playing golf?)

_____

_____

_____

_____

_____

_____

_____

CREATE A VISION BOARD

If you're a visual person, consider cutting out magazine pictures to create a collage of what you want your new life to look like. Place this vision board on a bulletin board or your refrigerator. Creating a sacred space that displays what you want brings it to life, especially if you place it somewhere you can see every day.

Visualization is one of the most powerful mind exercises you can do. But there's a secret to its success. Your board should focus on how you want to feel, not just on activities you want to partake in.

You can include 3 x 5 cards of your favorite Bible verses or motivational quotes, words that make you feel loved, valued, or rejuvenated. Place something there that makes you laugh.

The best part of creating a vision board is knowing that there are no rules. You can include anything you want and place them in any order. Make it fun. Make it all about you and what joy means to you.

If you know other moms who are going through the same recovery you are, invite them over for a vision board creation party.

Once your ALO sees that you're taking time for yourself, that you value yourself, he will respect you more, too. Maybe this will inspire him to create his own board. Wouldn't that be great?

As moms, we often feel tired, not because we've done too much, but because we have done too little of those things that spark in us.

Find your spark. Let's go blossom!

And the day came when the risk to remain tight in a bud was more painful than the risk it took to blossom.

—Jen Sincero

Flowering: Helping Others and Living a New Life.

Once the flower reaches blooming stage and gently opens its petals, we see its beauty and enjoy the blossoms. The bright colors attract visitors, like bees, to feast on the nectar. Worker-foraging bees collect nectar by sucking droplets with their straw-like tongues. Some of the nectar is stored in a special pouch in the bee's stomach until it gets back to the hive.

Once back at the hive, the nectar is regurgitated and processed into honey, a natural sweetener that we use on our food.

While collecting the nectar, bees carry pollen from bloom to bloom which stimulates the production of new seeds. Birds and wind then help disperse the seeds to new soil, and the lifecycle of seed-to-plant begins again.

Now that you have bloomed, and you're standing proud in your vibrant colors, you're able to carry the seeds of your fruits and labor into the lives of your family, other moms, and hopefully your addicted loved one. The more you recover and share your message with other moms who need your support, the more you'll be like the bees' honey, as you provide a sweeter life to those around you.

Congratulations! You'll be more effective in your job and as a parent, grandparent, and mom.

If you remember that you are the only person you can lead to do great things, you will know and live the true secret—your ability to master yourself will give you true power. When you find motivation to lead yourself well, others will follow.

My hope is that in the course of this guide, you've found hope in the exercises, in the support group, and in yourself.

Do you have everything figured out? Probably not. I know I don't, and I've been on this journey for a long, long time. Maybe more than ten years. We don't have to have it all figured out to keep going. We must keep growing.

Everything you've accomplished will not only help you, but it will help others you encounter. You'll be healthier, sturdier, more confident, and your fragrance will permeate to those around you. Moms will look at you and say, "I want what she has."

Michelle Weidenbenner

A word of warning: Flowers wilt and die unless they continue to surround themselves with water, sunshine, warmth, and the other nutrients they need to sustain life.

So must you.

Relapses happen, just like they will in your ALO in recovery. When your ALO struggles and you must sit by and wait for him to take the lead in his own life, it's tempting to help in the ineffective ways.

How will you continue to surround yourself with the skills, tools, and support that have helped you reach this step? What will you do to prevent a relapse in your own recovery? A relapse could be giving in to your ALO's manipulative demands, doing something for him that you said you wouldn't do, allowing yourself to be in his business instead of staying in yours.

Don't beat yourself up. All moms have done it too.

Make a list of those elements that have helped you keep your boundaries. Below are suggestions:

_____ Support group

_____ A hobby

_____ Exercise

_____ Proper sleep

_____ Meditation

_____ Accountability partner

_____ Volunteer

_____ Church group

_____ Reading about addiction recovery

_____ Training for recovery

_____ Other

_____

_____

_____

Continue implementing those things that are working for you and consider adding others too.

Michelle Weidenbenner

What do you want to add? To take care of yourself, you will need to be intentional, consistent, and passionate about your life. How will you maintain your growth so your efforts can exponentially multiply in other lives? Be specific with your list:

_____

_____

_____

_____

_____

_____

If you want to partner with a mom who will help you stay accountable, request an **accountability partner** at the Facebook page. Interview other moms to find out how they will support you. Choose someone you feel connected to. God will put the right person in your life, the person He feels you need at this point. Find someone who will encourage you, not judge you, but hold you accountable for doing those things you want to stay true to.

Even if you do relapse and help your child in a way you said you wouldn't, give yourself grace. Get back in your recovery mode.

"It is impossible to live without failing at something unless you live so cautiously that you might as well not have lived at all—in which case, you fail by default."

—J.K. Rowling

Look over your journal and the exercises in this book. Reflect. What worked? What went wrong? Where do you need help?

_____

_____

_____

_____

_____

_____

_____

_____

Talk to other moms who are working on their own recovery paths. What helps them?

_____

_____

_____

Michelle Weidenbenner

_____

_____

_____

There are no easy, clear-cut answers for how you should continue as a mom of an addicted loved one. You are doing the best you can do at this point in your life. Trust your heart. You know your child better than anyone.

"Through a long and painful process, I've learned that happiness is an inside job— not based on anything or anyone in the other material world. I've become a different and better person— not perfect, but still a work in progress."
—Alana Stewart

Your happiness is your inside job. Your ALO's happiness is *his* inside job.

Transformation happens when you choose a different life. See your ending. Will it to happen. Swap out the old lifestyle for a new one. Fight for a different life. You're worth it.

Spend at least fifteen more minutes journaling focusing on how you've bloomed and what you want your life to look like five years from now. Dream big. Let this flower be the example of the transformation you seek. The color represents petals of your vibrant willpower. Where are you in the story now? Where do you want to be? Visualize it.

_____

_____

_____

_____

_____

_____

_____

_____

_____

_____

Make your recovery louder than your addiction story. How will you do that? I'm doing that here with you because I'm all about making my mess a message to help others. I'm passionate about helping you to see the same truth. I hope you will loudly share your recovery story on the FB page so other moms can hear.

If we can help other moms to see the truth, to realize that we have a choice in how we respond to our ALO's choices, and that we can make a difference by finding joy in our lives first, wouldn't every mom want that? And wouldn't every ALO be inspired by a mom who could do that? I believe he or she could be.

I love to be around positive, joy-filled people. When I see them, I want what they have. Don't you? I want to surround myself with moms, like you, who are doing the hard work to heal, who are choosing a joy-filled life!

I need your story! Another way to get our messages out there and start a movement to stop our ALOs' using career is to write a collaborative book for moms from moms on *how to recover*.

If you're still reading this book (and many won't get this far) it means that you're serious about your recovery and changing the way you respond to your addicted loved one. Knowing that, I'd like to invite you to share your ***happily-ever-during*** story with me. This is different than your *happily-ever-after* because right now you can't be sure that your son or daughter will recover when you do. But you can't wait. You must march ahead on your journey because that's all you can control. It's possible you will have to recover while (*during*) they're *using*.

I'd like to publish the story of how you took control of your life despite your ALO's choices. Think how powerful this would be to moms who need to learn how to let go, but don't know how, or they're afraid. If they read the story of how you, and other moms, found joy, they will realize that they can transform too. You will bring them hope.

Please contact me if you're interested, and I'll send you the details. Don't worry if you don't think you write well. As an award-winning published author, I know a little about how to write and edit. It's the stories that matter. If we write with the intentions of helping other moms, our efforts will be for the right reasons, and bring glory to God.

Let me know about your transformation and what helped you succeed in letting go without giving up.

If you're interested in being included in this book, please send me an email with the words **Mighty Mom Book** in the subject line. That will get my attention!

I'll send you the guidelines.

I can't wait to hear your story and share it.

MY PRAYER FOR OUR RECOVERY
JOURNEY'S SUCCESS

Dear God,

Joy is something we moms of ALOs must fight for.

There will be days when we will feel awkward in our recovery. Letting go of our children is not easy because a mom's nature is to nurture. Letting go can feel cold and uncaring. We miss our children, the way they used to be, the way we related to each other, and the way we laughed when we were together.

Show us how letting go is a *loving* move, an action verb, and without action the chance of change in our child is lessened.

Help us to see that by changing the way we respond to our children we are giving them the freedom to experience their own journey.

We are hurting. Walk beside us to strengthen our faith in You, so we feel You near and hear Your voice.

Reveal our codependent behaviors to us so we can stop these behaviors that have become so ingrained and natural that we're unable to recognize them.

Remove Satan, who seeps into the trauma-wounded crevices of the souls of our children, so their hearts and souls will heal, too.

God, we know that we aren't in control of our children's lives, that we need to mind our own business, but this is tough. We've spent so much of our lives taking care of our children that taking care of ourselves doesn't feel right.

Show us that the reason we need to take care of ourselves is so our children will know that recovery is possible. We will be the hope our children need to see. Help us love ourselves even when it doesn't feel natural.

Give us patience to understand that we must practice new responses to get better. Recovery doesn't happen in a minute. It's not an event. It's a process. It might take years, but if we practice and pray, we will move into healthy habits that will strengthen our minds, hearts, and souls.

Some days, we won't want to work on our recovery. We'll lose hope. When that happens, embrace us with the warmth of Your protection, and guide us toward Your light.

Show us success for our endeavors and motivate us to want to continue to grow in our recovery. Growth needs to continue until we are with You in everlasting life.

Amen.

Michelle Weidenbenner

C O N T A C T   M E

Please let me know if this guidebook was helpful. Write to me at Michelle@MichelleWeidenbenner.com.

I'd love to know how I can further help you on your journey too. See you over at the Facebook page, MomsLettingGo.

Love and God Bless,
Michelle

SUGGESTED READING LIST

Beyond Addiction, How Science and Kindness Help People Change, by Jeffrey Foote, PHD, Carrie Wilkens, PHD, and Nicole Kosanke, PHD, with Stephanie Higgs.

Don't Let Your Kids Kill You, by Charles Rubin.

Loving What Is: Four Questions That Can Change Your Life, by Byron Katie.

Praying for the Prodigal: Encouragement and Practical Advice for Parents of Prodigals, by Andrea Merrell

Resisting Happiness, by Matthew Kelly.

Setting Boundaries with Your Adult Children, by Allison Bottke.

Smoke and Mirrors: The Magical World of Chemical Dependency, by Dorothy Marie England.

The Four Seasons of Recovery for Parents of Alcoholics and Addicts, by Michael Speakman, LISAC

The One-Minute Gratitude Journal, by Brenda Nathan.

You Are Not Alone: Hope for Hurting Parents of Troubled Kids, by Dena Yohe.

Made in the USA
Columbia, SC
20 November 2022

71810119R00069